THE SECRET ANNEX

THE SECRET ANNEX

ALIX SOBLER

The Secret Annex
first published 2015 by
Scirocco Drama
An imprint of J. Gordon Shillingford Publishing Inc.
© 2015 Alix Sobler

Scirocco Drama Editor: Glenda MacFarlane
Cover design by Terry Gallagher/Doowah Design Inc.
Cover photo by Mell Hattie, courtesy of ThinkStock
Author photo by luckygirl photography
Printed and bound in Canada on 100% post-consumer recycled paper.

We acknowledge the financial support of the Manitoba Arts Council and The Canada
Council for the Arts for our publishing program.

Library and Archives Canada Cataloguing in Publication

Sobler, Alix, 1978-, author
    The secret annex / Alix Sobler.

A play.
ISBN 978-1-927922-10-1 (pbk.)

    I. Title.

PS8637.O25S43 2015   C812'.6   C2015-900929-4

J. Gordon Shillingford Publishing
P.O. Box 86, RPO Corydon Avenue, Winnipeg, MB Canada R3M 3S3

The past is never dead. It's not even past.
—William Faulkner

For Anne and those like her, who remind us to ask the questions.

And for Jason, who has shown me the answer can be love.

Acknowledgements

I am so grateful to Steven Schipper, Camilla Holland, and Laurie Lam for supporting this project and bringing it to an audience. I am so lucky to have worked with the Playwrights Unit at the Prairie Theatre Exchange, and the many actors who participated in the readings and workshops. I would like to thank Heidi Malazdrewich for her dramaturgical support, direction and friendship. I am indebted to the cast of the original production for all their work and wisdom. So many individuals have aided me along the way in myriad roles, including John Kruizenga, Shana Gozansky, Elizabeth Gozansky, Trish Cooper, and many others. Much love to all my family and friends for their ongoing support.

Characters

Anne Frank – 25 at the start of the play
Margot Frank – 28 at the start of the play
Peter van Pels – 27 at the start of the play
Michael Stein – 40s at the start of the play
Virginia Belair – 40s at the start of the play

Setting

New York and Toronto
1955 and 1962

Production History

The Secret Annex premiered at the Royal Manitoba Theatre Centre, Winnipeg, on February 20, 2014 with the following cast and crew:

Anne Frank ....Tal Gottfried

Peter van Pels .... Andrew Cecon

Margot Frank .... Daria Puttaert

Virginia Belair .... Jennifer Lyon

Michael Stein .... Kevin Kruchkywich

Directed by Heidi Malazdrewich
Set and Costumes Design by Charlotte Dean
Lighting Design by Larry Isacoff
Sound Design by Mike Wright
Accent Design and Coaching by Shannon Vickers
Stage Management: Melissa Novecosky
Apprentice Stage Management: Airyn Lancaster

The Secret Annex was originally commissioned by the Winnipeg Jewish Theatre, and was written with support from the Manitoba Arts Council.

ALIX SOBLER

Alix Sobler

Originally from New York, Alix Sobler is a theatre artist who now splits her time between the United States and Canada. Her plays have been workshopped and produced at theatres across North America. She is a graduate of Brown University, and will receive her MFA in playwriting from Columbia University in 2017. She currently lives in New York City with her husband and two very creative cats.

Act I

Scene 1

1955.

> *ANNE is centre stage in a small pool of light. Behind her in shadows, PETER sits at a table. There are books. He is listening as she reads. While she reads, the lights slowly rise to reveal an apartment in Brooklyn.*

ANNE: *(Reading from the diary.)* "Yesterday evening, exiled government minister Balkesteyn spoke via the underground radio network about a plan to collect as many wartime diaries and letters as possible in order to create an anthology.

Of course, everybody made a dash for my diary. Imagine, how interesting it would be if I managed to publish a romantic novel about the Secret Annex; the title alone would have people believe it was a detective story..." Hmm.

PETER: What?

ANNE: Perhaps I should use that after all.

PETER: Go on.

ANNE: No, I think that's quite enough for today.

PETER: What? Why?

ANNE: Because, I have to write in this passage.

PETER: Well, read me something else then.

ANNE: You should be studying!

PETER: Why must you always be such a stickler?

ANNE: *(A pause.)* I remember grandmother. Braiding my hair.

             PETER doesn't respond. Looks back at his books.

             Peter.

PETER: What?

ANNE: I said, Grandmother. Braiding my hair. Smelling of basil and oil. *(Pause.)*

             You're turn.

PETER: I'm studying. *(She looks at him with an impatient, mischievous look. He thinks.)* I remember the gymnasium.

ANNE: More. What about it?

PETER: The floors after they'd been waxed. In your socks, you could take a running start and slide for ages.

ANNE: Good one.

PETER: Your turn.

ANNE: I remember Moortje. Soft and warm and purring away. *(Beat.)* Poor Moortje.

             He tries to sneak a look at her pages, but she pulls them away.

PETER: Let me see the new pages.

ANNE: No!

PETER: Well why not?

ANNE: Because…you can't read them out of context.

PETER: Out of context? Impossible! I was there when it happened.

ANNE: You can read them later, when I have the new draft. In the meantime, we're playing "I Remember". Now come on.

PETER: Mouschi.

ANNE: I just did a cat!

PETER: So? Does it mean I can't remember my cat? Mouschi. Sleepy eyed and kneading my chest. Your turn.

ANNE: Hm…I remember the tree. Through the skylight.

PETER: Before only. You're cheating.

MARGOT enters, takes off her hat and coat.

MARGOT: Hello.

ANNE: Margot! We're playing "I Remember". Join us!

MARGOT: Again? You know, the whole world is out there, and you can go see it! Games like "I Remember" were for…before.

ANNE: Nonsense. I love to remember.

MARGOT: Mail, Anne.

MARGOT hands ANNE a few letters which ANNE takes, but doesn't really look at.

Hello Peter. Nice to see you here. Again.

PETER: Hello Margot.

MARGOT: How are Hermann and Auguste? Enjoying life up north?

PETER: Yes, it seems so. Toronto suits them.

MARGOT: And how is Betty?

PETER: She's fine.

> *A tiny awkward pause.*

ANNE: Come on, Margot! What do you remember? About the old times?

MARGOT: Hardly anything.

ANNE: Come now.

MARGOT: It's true.

ANNE: Polar bears!

PETER: Pardon?

ANNE: I remember the day we learned about polar bears because I thought a white bear was just about the most spectacular thing I had ever heard of. A white bear! Magic! But Malka Feinberg wore a white dress that day the poor thing, she was a rather large girl, and after school the boys made a circle around her and were teasing her for being a polar bear. So I got into the middle of that circle and planted a big kiss on her cheek and said how much I love polar bears and how I think they are about the most spectacular thing on the planet!

> *Pause.*

PETER: How can one compete with you at the game of "I Remember"?

MARGOT: Really Anne.

ANNE: OK Margot, your turn.

> *ANNE begins to open her letters, absentmindedly.*

PETER: She doesn't have to play if she doesn't want to.

ANNE:	Fiddlesticks! We have nothing left from those days, except a handful of pictures and my diary. Think of it as research for my book.
PETER:	Ah, the book.
MARGOT:	Indeed the book. I am so surprised that has come up.
ANNE:	All right.
PETER:	Are you writing a book Anne? I had no idea.
MARGOT:	Yes, do go on about that.
ANNE:	Just one Margot? What are you afraid of? "I remember..."
MARGOT:	I remember a call-up notice and that is all. A man at the door telling me to report, and nothing else. *(Beat.)* Why must we always be remembering? Why can't we just look ahead?
	A moment. ANNE looks at her mail and then suddenly jumps up.
ANNE:	Oh my goodness.
PETER:	What is it?
MARGOT:	What's the matter?
ANNE:	It's from Berger & Simmons. Berger & Simmons! The publishing house where I sent my book!
MARGOT:	What?
PETER:	And?
ANNE:	*(Scanning the letter for information.)* And...the Senior Executive I spoke to has read the book, and would like a meeting to discuss the work!
MARGOT:	Oh my!

ANNE: Virginia Belair!

MARGOT: Who's that?

ANNE: See? She signed the letter.

PETER: Virginia Belair. Sounds like a movie star!

MARGOT: Well is that good?

ANNE: Is it good? How can it not be good?

MARGOT: I don't know, I don't know how these things work—

ANNE: It must mean they're going to publish it! I knew it! I knew it would happen. All those years, hiding… this is what it was all for! *(She hugs PETER.)* Peter. Can you believe it?

PETER: Of course I can!

ANNE: And now…now it will be published and…and… and we can all take a trip!

MARGOT: A trip?

PETER: Where shall we go?

ANNE: We'll go…we'll go to Paris!

MARGOT: UGH!

PETER: Anywhere but Europe. Please.

ANNE: Of course. Then…we'll go to Israel.

MARGOT: No thank you.

PETER: Too hot.

ANNE: OK, fine. We'll go to the South Pole to see the polar bears!

PETER: I don't think there are polar bears at the South Pole.

ANNE: Well, then the North Pole. Wherever they are, that's where we are going! Now we'll have some more money Margot, perhaps you and George can set a date for the wedding!

MARGOT: Oh, Anne, do you think?

ANNE: Why not? Once my memoir is published I can write all the time. I'll be able to move out, get my own place...you and George will take a proper honeymoon—

PETER: To the South Pole!

ANNE: Margot, don't you see? Everything is going just as it should. Everything happens for a reason.

MARGOT: Yes, perhaps you are right.

            They hug. ANNE gestures to PETER to join them. They all hug.

            I think a toast is in order!

            She breaks away to go get the alcohol.

ANNE: Yes, Let's drink champagne!

PETER: Champagne. Fancy!

MARGOT: I'm afraid all we have is a bit of schnapps.

ANNE: That's perfect.

PETER: Let's have a drink then. To love!

            They look at him.

PETER: To Margot and George's wedding!

MARGOT: To Anne's book!

ANNE: To us! To the rest of our lives. May they be long and full of happiness. Thank you God for bringing us to this season! Isn't it wonderful that we didn't die? I am so grateful for the way things turned out. Forget how we would have suffered. Imagine what we would have missed! L'Chaim!

PETER &
MARGOT: L'Chaim!

> *They drink. Laugh.*

> *The lights shift and VIRGINIA enters. She joins ANNE at the window.*

Scene 2

> *VIRGINIA BELAIR's office in the Berger & Simmons Publishing House, on the East Side. VIRGINIA sits reviewing manuscripts.*

VIRGINIA: Hell of a view isn't it?

ANNE: Oh, yes.

VIRGINIA: You have no idea how many hours I had to work to get a view like that. A lot more hours than any of the boys in the house I can tell you. You got any brothers?

ANNE: Not really.

VIRGINIA: Not really?

ANNE: Well there's Peter. He's practically my brother. But in reality it's just me and Margot.

VIRGINIA: Right, right of course, Margot. And Peter. Stupid question. I know everything about you now, don't I?

ANNE: Well. I don't know about—

VIRGINIA: Well sweetheart, I can tell you right now that no man would have had to work as hard as I did to get where I am today. Not that they don't work hard, in their own way, but they haven't a clue what it means to be a woman in this world, you hear me?

ANNE: Yes. I can hear you.

VIRGINIA: Please sit down. Thanks for coming Miss Frank—

ANNE: Please, call me Anne.

VIRGINIA: All right, Anne—

ANNE: It's my pleasure. I was so excited to get your letter—

VIRGINIA: Cigarette?

ANNE: ...no thank you.

VIRGINIA: No?

ANNE: No, I don't smoke.

VIRGINIA: You should start.

ANNE: Should I?

VIRGINIA: Absolutely! It's a wonderful habit. It gives you something to bond with other people about. It gives you something to do with your hands in every situation. And it's quite sophisticated. When I was a girl my mother would have died before getting caught with a cigarette. But nowadays all the high society ladies smoke. Imagine how times have changed! How old are you?

ANNE: Twenty-five.

VIRGINIA: Right, right. It's in the book. I forget I have a handbook to all your secrets.

ANNE: Well, I don't know if I would—

VIRGINIA: You sure you don't want a cigarette?

ANNE: No, thank you.

VIRGINIA: Suit yourself. *(She lights her cigarette.)* Now, what was I saying?

ANNE: You were saying…

VIRGINIA: Hm?

ANNE: About my memoir?

VIRGINIA: Oh yes of course. Well, Miss Frank…Anne. Anne? Anne. Unfortunately I don't have very good news for you.

ANNE: Well I…what?

VIRGINIA: Yes, well I'm sorry to be the one to tell you, we're passing on your memoir.

ANNE: What?

VIRGINIA: Yes, we're passing. *(Louder.)* Passing. Vetoed. *(Pause.)* It's gonna be a "no".

ANNE: Oh.

VIRGINIA: I am sure you are disappointed.

ANNE: Well, yes. Yes I thought—the letter—

VIRGINIA: The thing is, it's just not what we're looking for right now.

ANNE: Not what you're looking for? But I don't understand. When I first contacted you, you said…you said the company was so eager to publish first hand accounts of the war.

VIRGINIA: Yes that's true.

ANNE: And then when I got the letter, I just assumed—

VIRGINIA: Well yes cherish, about the war. The real war that was happening out there. The battlefields. The front lines. You can't believe the stories coming out of Poland—well I don't need to tell you. People on the brink of death. On the brink of humanity! Unfathomable cruelty and pain. It makes for incredible reading.

ANNE: I see.

VIRGINIA: Your book is just a little…what's the word?

ANNE: Painless?

VIRGINIA: Exactly. (ANNE *flinches*.) Oh, listen sister, I don't mean to belittle what you and your people went through. I am sure it was awful…in its own way. I know it was, I read the book on it. All I'm saying is, it's hard to compete with death marches and crematoriums. And that's the stuff the boys upstairs are looking for.

ANNE: Upstairs?

VIRGINIA: You know the big cheese. Head honchos. The men in charge.

ANNE: Yes of course.

VIRGINIA: There just needs to be a bit more of a story. More of a payoff for this sort of thing to sell.

ANNE: A payoff?

VIRGINIA: A little more blood, a little more romance. Maybe a laugh or two. There's just not enough happening here I am afraid.

ANNE: But…this is what happened.

VIRGINIA: That doesn't mean it's going to make a good book.

ANNE: But…are you sure people want that? My family doesn't even like to discuss the war. Are you sure people are really ready to delve into the camps, the gas chambers?

VIRGINIA: Look, it's not my cup of tea, but it seems to be what people are interested in.

ANNE: But. Then, why have you asked me here? Why not just put this in the letter?

VIRGINIA: Yes! That's the good news! I wanted to see you, to meet with you face to face because I think you have potential.

ANNE: Oh. I am willing to work with an editor. I understand some parts might need some finessing.

VIRGINIA: That sounds like a grand idea.

ANNE: Yes?

VIRGINIA: Yes, absolutely. You write on, find someone to help you shape it into more of a story, maybe some twists and turns.

ANNE: And you will help me do that?

VIRGINIA: Well, no, sweetheart, we are passing on the book. As it is now. But you bring me back a boffo socko rewrite, and I might just be able to sell it. No promises mind you. It's hard to revisit a project that's already been passed over.

ANNE: But I can't possibly afford to pay an editor on my own. My sister is getting married, as it is I can barely—

VIRGINIA: You don't have to tell me love, things are tough all around. But we can't be paying editors to work on books all over the town or where would we be? *(ANNE looks utterly defeated.)* Listen honey, the writing is good. But so much of this book is so... dark. So depressing. You're a kid! Lighten up!

ANNE: Lighten...up?

VIRGINIA: Sure!

ANNE: But it's about being in hiding.

VIRGINIA: OK, but that doesn't mean it has to be all doom and gloom does it?

ANNE: But there are people writing about the camps. You said yourself—

VIRGINIA: *(Darkly.)* Stop telling me what I said. I hate it when people do that. *(Pause.)* Listen, sweetie, those are men. Men are the ones writing about the camps. Men can suffer. Suffer and survive. Suffer and survive and thrive even. We like that. They're strong. They're serious. They're the best in all of us. But a girl? A teenage girl? Locked in an attic, complaining about hunger, kissing the boy next door...and then losing interest! *(Quietly.)* And all this talk of kissing other girls? Of all the things!

ANNE: But that's just who I am.

VIRGINIA: Well honey, that may be true, but it's just not something I can sell. You know they put us together because, well as the only woman in the building they hand me a lot of the newbies but—well I have to be careful what I fight for, they're always looking for a reason to axe the skirt, you see. And, well. There's just not enough here.

           Pause.

ANNE: So if I am to understand you—the camps— Auschwitz, Sobibor—those stories are good.

VIRGINIA: That's right.

ANNE: As long as it's a man.

VIRGINIA: Now you're listening.

ANNE: And my story, about the attic, that's too dark.

           Pause.

VIRGINIA: Listen puppy, you've got to look at the big picture
                 here. You know, you tried. This was a good effort.
                 You just didn't knock it out of the park, that's all.
                 You just need to keep writing.

ANNE: The park?

VIRGINIA: It's a baseball reference. You'll want to learn a few
                 of those if you plan on staying in Brooklyn. All I'm
                 saying is—you've got talent. Maybe a lot of it. There
                 may be a great story in you. Hell, there may be a
                 great story in here. But I haven't seen it yet kid. So,
                 better luck next time. Put it aside for a while. Write
                 something else. Then come back to it and you'll see
                 you can do better. Now I hate to cut things short,
                 but I've got a few things to do if I want to keep this
                 view.

                 ANNE goes to say something else to VIRGINIA,
                 but the meeting is clearly over as VIRGINIA,
                 already distracted by the next task, exits.

                 ANNE stands for a moment, stung. The stage
                 becomes her apartment and as she turns she sees
                 PETER there, waiting.

Scene 3

                 ANNE and MARGOT's Brooklyn apartment.
                 PETER sees ANNE as she enters.

PETER: What happened at the meeting? What did they
                 say?

ANNE: Oh. Well. Things don't happen as quickly as one
                 would hope in the publishing world. They are still
                 very interested, very compelled by the memoir. It's
                 just...well...

PETER: Oh.

ANNE: They don't want it. Not as it is.

PETER: No. It's not possible!

ANNE: She said only with a rewrite, a complete and total rewrite. I don't understand. I thought people would care about this story.

PETER: They will! It's only one rejection.

ANNE: I suppose. But perhaps everyone will say the same thing.

PETER: And what is that?

ANNE: That it's...it's not interesting enough. I am beginning to think that you and I are the only two people in the world who will be interested in it. I just don't understand how something that was so terrifying to live through can end up being so boring when you write it down.

PETER: It's not boring Anne.

ANNE: I suppose if I had been a great beauty... Or if there was a tragic ending, then they could have put my picture on it and sold it all over the world. But it seems that having me here, having me show up in the publisher's office with my inexpensive shoes and European face...it takes all the romance from the memoir. Perhaps I should just write something else. Get back to my stories. Perhaps work on some fiction. But I just know that this is the story. This is the one that will help me make my mark. Oh, what does she know anyway? These American women. They are so, so...dreadful aren't they?

PETER: I don't know. Some of them are alright.

ANNE: Of course how silly of me. How is Betty?

PETER: Well. Very well. At least I hope.

ANNE: Oh? And why is that then?

PETER: Well, I've just come from making a purchase.

ANNE: A purchase? How mysterious. What sort of purchase?

PETER: A diamond as a matter of fact.

ANNE: A diamond? Whatever for? *(Pause.)* Peter van Pels... what are you saying? Are you...are you going to get married?

PETER: If she says yes.

ANNE: Oh. Oh my. *(ANNE sits as though the wind has been knocked out of her.)*

PETER: Anne, are you alright?

ANNE: Yes, yes of course. Just...a lot of surprises for one day.

PETER: Shall I get you a glass of water?

ANNE: No. No I am alright. Come. Sit next to me.

              PETER sits next to her.

              Why have you suddenly decided to do this?

PETER: Is it sudden? I don't know. Betty and I have known each other nearly a year. I've grown quite fond of her.

ANNE: Fond of her? But Peter.

PETER: Yes?

ANNE: To marry someone, don't you think you should love her?

PETER: Come on. That's child's talk. There are many reasons to be married.

ANNE: Are there?

PETER: You yourself have always said your parents didn't marry for love.

ANNE: *(Rises, thinking.)* What do Hermann and Auguste say?

PETER: I haven't told them yet.

ANNE: You haven't discussed it with your parents?

PETER: They've met Betty. They quite like her.

ANNE: Well of course your mother would prefer her. Betty's so quiet and deferential.

PETER: Prefer her to whom?

> *ANNE says nothing for a moment.*

Well. Your enthusiasm is overwhelming.

ANNE: I'm sorry. Congratulations. *(Silence. Trying to muster up some excitement:)* May I see the ring?

PETER: You want to see the ring?

ANNE: Well yes, if you don't mind.

> *After a moment, he hands her the diamond.*

It's very beautiful.

PETER: I thought so.

ANNE: What are you going to say? To Betty?

PETER: I don't know. I hadn't thought about it.

ANNE: Hadn't thought about it? Well you best get to thinking man! She's going to be telling this story to all her friends, family, not to mention the countless generations you are going to produce in your very manly way.

PETER: Thank you. Now I am much less nervous.

ANNE: Well, let's rehearse.

              ANNE hands the ring back to him and gestures for him to practice.

PETER: Oh Anne. You and your games.

ANNE: No games! I just want you to think it through.

              After a moment, PETER gets down on one knee, opens the ring box and looks at ANNE with great earnestness.

PETER: Will you marry me?

ANNE: *(Pause.)* Dreadful.

PETER: Why is that dreadful?

ANNE: Well, could you manage to be more unoriginal?

PETER: I didn't realize originality was so important in such a thing.

ANNE: But Peter—

PETER: Why don't you just write something out? You're the one who's always good with words, I've never been.

ANNE: Don't be silly. No, it has to come from you.

PETER: Well from me, "Will you marry me?" is enough.

ANNE: Well I suppose a girl who would say yes to that sort of proposal won't be too bothered about the whole question of whether you love her or not.

PETER: Why are you being this way?

ANNE: If you can't think of the right way to propose, do you suppose it's a sign that maybe you shouldn't be getting married?

PETER: What do you want from me?

ANNE: I want you to—

PETER: What? To what?

ANNE: Nothing! Nothing.

PETER: *(He looks at her a moment.)* I think I should go. *(He starts to leave.)*

ANNE: Wait! Not yet. I'm sorry. This is a change. That's all. More change. I'll get used to it.

PETER: It was silly of me to come here.

ANNE: No, Peter! Not silly at all. Imagine if I had gotten a phone call from you! It would have been a dreadful disappointment. And you know how I hate to be the last to know. So much the better to get this news in person. Don't go angry. Please. Let's have a dance shall we?

PETER: A dance?

ANNE: Yes! A celebratory dance.

PETER: I don't know.

          She puts on a record, "Tennessee Waltz" by Patti Page.

ANNE: May I have this dance?

PETER: Certainly.

          They dance quietly for a moment.

ANNE: Will you be married before you finish school then?

PETER: Long before.

ANNE: Is that right?

PETER: I've left school.

ANNE: What?

PETER: It's not practical.

ANNE: But, medical school—

PETER: There are just so many more years of study left. I've
              decided to go into business.

ANNE: I see.

PETER: I've thought through it. This is the best thing. Betty
              will want children right away of course, and it
              won't do for me to be in school.

                      *They look at each other a moment. Then they
                      continue to dance.*

ANNE: I remember, Peter.

PETER: What do you remember Anne?

ANNE: I remember when all you wanted to be was a
              carpenter.

PETER: I remember when you used to irritate me incessantly.
              And you were in love with Peter Schiff.

ANNE: I remember when you explained the birds and the
              bees to me.

PETER: Oh my. Were we ever really that young?

                      Pause.

ANNE: Do you remember the attic?

PETER: *(With a sigh.)* I thought we were only supposed to
              talk about before.

ANNE: I know. *(Beat.)* It was awful wasn't it?

PETER: It was.

ANNE: Look at us now. You, about to be married. Margot
              about to be married.

PETER: And what about you Anne? What will you do now that the book is not being published?

ANNE: Yet.

PETER: Yet.

ANNE: I'll need to make some money. I will have to get a job, rent a room somewhere I suppose.

PETER: I thought that the book would be published. That you'd be touring the world. I thought you'd have forgotten me by next month.

ANNE: Peter! What a thing to say.

PETER: I suppose if you married me, you wouldn't have to work. I would support you.

ANNE: Lucky Betty.

PETER: Maybe she is lucky. Maybe you should think about it.

              He tips her head up to look at him.

ANNE: What are you saying?

              He looks at her. He kisses her. She pulls away.

              Peter!

PETER: I know you said you didn't feel that way…then. But now, now there's been time, and don't you see? Don't you see how we belong together?

ANNE: But what about Betty?

              He kisses her again. She is less resistant this time. From off stage we hear MARGOT:

MARGOT: Oh, Anne you've left your keys in the door again.

              ANNE and PETER pull apart as she enters. She can sense something was happening.

MARGOT:	Hello. *(She looks at the record player.)* Have I interrupted a dance? I'm sorry.
ANNE:	We are celebrating.
MARGOT:	Oh? Anne, your meeting!
ANNE:	No, no, not me.
MARGOT:	But what about the book?
ANNE:	No, not yet. It's Peter. Peter is getting married.

> *ANNE goes to change the music. MARGOT crosses to PETER.*

MARGOT:	Really?
PETER:	Maybe.
ANNE:	To Betty, of course.
PETER:	Well. Thinking about it.
MARGOT:	Well. *(Looking back and forth between them.)* Isn't that something? Mazel tov Peter.
PETER:	Thank you. It's not official yet.
ANNE:	That music was too sad! I found something else.
PETER:	You have quite the collection don't you Anne?
MARGOT:	Peter, are you alright? You seem flushed.
PETER:	I'm fine. I'm wonderful.

> *"Rag Mop" by the Ames Brothers starts to play.*

PETER:	Oh my! I wouldn't know the first thing about how to dance to this.
ANNE:	Come I'll show you!

> *They dance. At first they are awkward, but ANNE*

wears him down after a minute. They are breathless and laughing. As they dance:

MARGOT: Just ask her how she learned to dance that way!

PETER: I don't suppose I want to know!

ANNE: Oh yes, I live a scandalous life of dance halls and shady men. How else am I to collect stories for all my future books?

PETER: What about you Margot? Join us?

MARGOT: I couldn't possibly.

ANNE: There will be plenty of time to dance at your wedding, won't there be Margot?

MARGOT: Yes, I suppose I won't be able to get out of it then, will I? Why don't I get some schnapps? Another toast. To Peter's upcoming engagement.

           After MARGOT as she exits.

PETER: Well, just…to weddings in general! *(Back at ANNE.)* To whomever we end up with.

ANNE: All those lucky devils.

           PETER and ANNE continue to dance for a bit. MARGOT interrupts and pulls ANNE toward MICHAEL's office. She fusses over her appearance, nervously making sure she looks "right". MICHAEL appears on the phone.

Scene 4

           MICHAEL STEIN's office.

MICHAEL: *(On the phone.)* No, no Gilbert, I already told you now is the time to make the big move! Forget about him, he's dead in the water. Mark my words in a month's time he'll be belly up. If we move now we're sitting pretty.

A knock. MARGOT peeks in.

MARGOT: Anne is here.

> *MICHAEL nods and waves her in. ANNE enters and looks back at MARGOT, unsure. MARGOT shoos her in and closes the door behind her.*

MICHAEL: Uh-huh. Is it a risk? Sure it is. Will it pay off? Damn straight. Have I ever steered you wrong before? Hey I told you to dance with her, not to marry her, you old dog. *(Laughs.)* Speaking of... I have to go Gilbert, there's a girl here about the receptionist position. Angela got married. Margot is getting married. I know, well serves me right for hiring the pretty ones. *(He looks at ANNE. He slowly hangs up.)* My apologies for that.

ANNE: Not at all.

MICHAEL: Please have a seat.

> *She sits.*

I'm Mr. Stein.

ANNE: A pleasure.

MICHAEL: Please call me Michael.

ANNE: OK, Michael. I'm Anne Frank. Margot's sister.

MICHAEL: Yes! Pleasure to meet you Miss Frank. Margot tells me you are quite the writer.

ANNE: I am.

MCHAEL: Modest too I see.

> *She smiles politely. Pause.*

MICHAEL: That was a joke.

ANNE: Oh. Well. I always think this prizing of modesty is an American habit, left over from your Puritanical heritage.

MICHAEL: Well I can assure you my Puritanical heritage is limited. *(Pause.)* I'm Jewish.

ANNE: Of course.

MICHAEL: As you would know, we are not known for prudishness.

ANNE: Even so, I think being in America long enough, it seeps into your blood.

MICHAEL: I see. Well we're going to miss Margot around here. We are very happy for her, but very sorry to see her go I can tell you that. If you are anything like her we could really use you.

ANNE: Oh. But I'm not.

MICHAEL: Not what?

ANNE: Anything like Margot.

MICHAEL: Oh.

ANNE: I'm sorry.

MICHAEL: Well how many words to do you type a minute?

ANNE: No, I don't know how to type.

MICHAEL: You don't know how to type?

ANNE: I am certain I can figure it out. The letters are on the keys, correct?

MICHAEL: Yes.

ANNE: I'm not worried about it then.

MICHAEL: Mm-hm. And how are you with numbers?

ANNE: I'm afraid I am dreadful with numbers.

MICHAEL: Really!

ANNE: Oh yes, math has always been my worst subject.

MICHAEL: I see. Well what have you done at your other jobs?

ANNE: I've never had a job.

MICHAEL: Never…had a job.

ANNE: Not as of yet. We were displaced for a long time after the war, and since then I have just been fixing up my English, learning about America, trying to… fit in.

MICHAEL: Of course…I understand you girls have had a rough time of it.

He rises and crosses away from his desk.

ANNE: We had our troubles during the war. So did everyone else it seems.

MICHAEL: I wasn't able to serve, myself. Flat feet.

ANNE: Flat feet? I don't see how that would prevent you from shooting at Germans.

MICHAEL: *(Amused.)* No, I guess it wouldn't, but I don't make the rules. Even so, I believed in helping with the war effort. And we're helping now, through the firm. Helping survivors find jobs, places to live… When the stories came out about what was going on over there…well. Margot didn't want to talk about it much, but I've figured out some. Locked in an attic for three years. That must have been… never mind, I'm sure you don't want to discuss it.

ANNE: Oh, I have no problem discussing it. I've written a book about it.

MICHAEL: Have you?

ANNE: Yes. *(Remembering.)* But Margot told me not to bring it up.

MICHAEL: And why's that?

ANNE: I have a habit of talking too much. Since I was a child. You see I am rewriting the book and I tend to find it quite consuming. *(ANNE crosses to his desk and takes her manuscript out of her bag.)* When it comes up I end up talking about it, incessantly. But this book is my life! I probably shouldn't be looking for a job at all. It will be too distracting from my writing. But with Margot getting married I will need to support myself. I refuse to be dependent on any man. And anyway, perhaps getting out, finding a position will give me more to write about. I haven't found many subjects since coming to America. But of course I'm really focusing on rewrites right now. I won't be writing anything new, not until The Attic sells. That's the name! Of my memoir. It's based on the diary I kept during the war, Kitty. *(She pulls Kitty, and the memoir out of her bag.)* I'm on my sixth draft of *The Attic*. *(She frowns, thinking about it.)* Actually, recently I've been thinking of changing the name. Something I thought up a long time ago. Maybe, *The Secret Annex*. I've always thought adding the word "secret" makes something more intriguing to a reader, don't you think so? *(He goes to answer her but she doesn't give him the chance.)* I wonder how much a title matters sometimes. It's not really fair. You spend years and years writing a thing, pour your heart and soul into it, and then you are damned because you pick the wrong title. Too obscure. Or too literal. It's so hard to know. *The Secret Annex*. I mean does it promise something it can't deliver, or does it entice you just enough? *(Pause. ANNE clears her throat.)* I am not supposed to talk about my book.

MICHAEL: Of course not. *(Pause. He considers her.)*

ANNE: But I need the work. And so if the offer is made, I will accept the job. *(She, now behind his desk, sits in his chair.)*

MICHAEL: Well Anne, I just have one more question for you. *(Resigned to defeat, he sits in the chair she started in.)* Do you see yourself getting married anytime soon?

ANNE: No sir!

MICHAEL: Well, then you're hired. Please give your information to Gladys at the front and she will arrange for your cheques. It's $40 a week and I don't tolerate tardiness.

ANNE: Yes, sir. Thank you.

MICHAEL: Mondays are partner meetings. You will have to take minutes. Otherwise you will just be answering the phones and taking memos for me. It's really not complicated stuff. You seem smart.

ANNE: Yes, I am.

MICHAEL: And obviously candour won't be a problem. *(Pause.)* We'll have to work on that sense of humour though.

ANNE: Oh, I'm sorry! I am still learning the peculiarities of the language. Upstairs boys and hitting things in parks.

MICHAEL: *(He looks at her and smiles.)* Not to worry. We'll get you all caught up. That will be all.

        ANNE goes to leave.

Oh and Anne?

ANNE: Yes?

MICHAEL: I'd like to read your book sometime. If you'd let me.

ANNE: Yes? Well, it's not finished. I need an editor.

MICHAEL: I'm a good reader. I can be very objective.

ANNE: Well…maybe. Once we've gotten to know each other a bit better, perhaps.

MICHAEL: I look forward to that.

> *ANNE puts her hand out to shake. He takes it. They shake hands.*

> *As the lights come down, MICHAEL pulls ANNE into a playful slow dance. "My Love" by Little Willie John plays as they dance, and eventually strip down to their undergarments and the stage around them becomes MICHAEL's apartment.*

Scene 5

> *ANNE and MICHAEL in bed. He is reading her book. She is hovering about him.*

MICHAEL: Please stop.

ANNE: Oh you're at that bit. It needs some tightening, I know.

MICHAEL: Stop it.

ANNE: I am just saying, you can't judge the ending by that bit, it needs work, and I am aware of this.

MICHAEL: Miss Frank, would you let me read for goodness sake?

> *ANNE wanders around the apartment in her slip. MICHAEL chuckles at something.*

ANNE: What?

He shoots her a dirty look and continues reading. She pulls out a magazine and absentmindedly thumbs through it. He sighs. She looks at him. He ignores her. Finally, MICHAEL turns the last page.

MICHAEL: Finished.

ANNE: *(Turning around.)* Well?

MICHAEL: Well you are a terrible typist.

ANNE: Michael—

MICHAEL: Can't believe I hired you as a secretary. It's riddled with mistakes.

ANNE: Michael—

MICHAEL: It's beautiful.

ANNE: Really?

MICHAEL: Really. It's poignant, heartbreaking, hopeful… Just lovely.

ANNE: Oh what a relief!

MICHAEL: But Anne…

ANNE: What?

MICHAEL: It's so personal.

ANNE: Well, yes, it's a memoir.

MICHAEL: But there are so many things in it that…are you sure you want the public knowing such things? Your relationship with your mother. Your sexual fantasies.

ANNE: I thought you would like those bits.

MICHAEL: I like all your bits. But do you really want to share them with the world?

ANNE: This is the story. Besides, at this point, I've worked on it so much…it's all been rewritten so many times, in a way it hardly feels like me anymore.

MICHAEL: Oh it's you alright.

ANNE: What do you mean?

MICHAEL: This is your soul, Anne Frank. Every inch of this book is you. It's your selfishness, your stubbornness, your naiveté.

ANNE: You flatter me.

MICHAEL: And also your exuberance, your wisdom, your beauty… But, I just don't know if you want this out there, leaving you so vulnerable.

ANNE: What are you getting at?

MICHAEL: Have you ever considered, just think about it, turning it into a novel?

ANNE: A novel?

MICHAEL: Well yes. Fictionalizing it. It would give you the freedom to change some of what happened, add more drama to the story. You could bring it back to the publisher with a whole new approach, might spark their interest. And it would allow you to change the names.

ANNE: What names?

MICHAEL: In the book.

ANNE: Why should that matter?

MICHAEL: I am just thinking about your reputation.

ANNE: And why should you care about that? You had no trouble at all bedding me despite my being far, far younger than you.

MICHAEL: That's true.

ANNE: Nor were you deterred by the fact that I am your subordinate in our work place.

MICHAEL: And I probably would have fired you weeks ago had we not been schtupping.

ANNE: Michael!

MICHAEL: Well you don't type well.

ANNE: And you don't seem to mind carrying on this affair for three months, completely in secret, I am keeping it from my parents, from my sister and my dearest friends. Why should you then suddenly care about my reputation?

MICHAEL: I just want to marry a girl with a good reputation that's all.

ANNE: *(Pause.)* What?

MICHAEL: I mean, I will know you are a depraved and wanton sexual deviant. But as long as I am the only one who knows it, I have no problem getting married. In fact all the better.

ANNE: What are you saying?

MICHAEL: Anne Frank. Will you marry me?

             A moment. She runs and kisses him.

ANNE: Is this a joke? Or a language misunderstanding?

MICHAEL: I don't think so. What else could "will you marry me" possibly mean?

ANNE: It's only been three months!

MICHAEL: I knew the day I met you.

             She kisses him again.

	Is that a yes?
ANNE:	Hold on a minute. What about the book?
MICHAEL:	Here, I'll move it.
ANNE:	No I mean, my writing. Will I be able to pursue my writing? I have to have my book published.
MICHAEL:	What kind of a question is that? Of course.
ANNE:	*(She pulls away for a moment.)* What will be expected of me?
MICHAEL:	Expected of you? This isn't a job interview. I want to marry you. I want us to have a life, children.
ANNE:	*(She looks at him.)* Children.
MICHAEL:	Well, yes of course. You want children don't you?
ANNE:	Yes.
MICHAEL:	I want little Annes running around the house. Scowling at every silly thing I say. Their noses buried in books. Telling me all the things they learned that day, all of the things I must understand this very minute. Little Annes.

She pulls away from him. Goes back to the dressing table. A darkness has fallen.

What is it?

ANNE:	I don't know. Children? More children? In this world?
MICHAEL:	It's the only place we can have them.
ANNE:	It's a terrible place sometimes.
MICHAEL:	And a wonderful place other times.

She says nothing.

Anne. We'll protect them.

ANNE: Well, we'll certainly try to won't we?

MICHAEL: You love me, don't you?

ANNE: In a way that I didn't know was possible.

MICHAEL: Then what is it?

ANNE: It's just—well, I can't be just an ordinary housewife and mother Michael. I need more than that.

MICHAEL: Yes, Miss Frank. I read your book.

ANNE: Alright then. Ask me again in a year.

Happy again, she gets up and begins to dress.

MICHAEL: You want me to ask again in a year?

ANNE: I can't be too distracted just now. Things are right, just the way they are.

MICHAEL: Things are right for you.

ANNE: What's the matter Mr. Stein? Can't you wait that long?

MICHAEL: I've waited my whole life for someone like you. I can wait another year.

MICHAEL gathers his things to get dressed.

ANNE: Good. I'll let you know.

MICHAEL: Let me know what?

ANNE: When you can re-propose.

MICHAEL: Oh. Well I look forward to it. And your parents?

ANNE: Yes?

MICHAEL: I'll meet them?

ANNE: Of course! But not just yet.

MICHAEL: Anne.

ANNE: Just a bit more time.

MICHAEL: What about Margot's wedding?

ANNE: What about it?

MICHAEL: That would be a lovely time to meet them. To meet everyone.

ANNE: Oh I don't know. You'll be dreadfully bored.

MICHAEL: Bored at a Jewish wedding? When the bride and her sister are both dear to me?

ANNE: Michael, it's just...I am not sure yet how to tell people.

MICHAEL: People. You mean Peter?

ANNE: I said no such thing.

MICHAEL: But you forget. I read your book.

ANNE: Let's not talk about Peter.

MICHAEL: Agreed. Let's never speak of him again.

ANNE: Stop that. He's like family to me. You'll have to get used to it.

MICHAEL: Do you love him?

ANNE: Of course I love him. He's like my brother.

MICHAEL: That is not what I meant.

ANNE: He is a boy for whom I had great affection, and still do. But not love. Not like I feel for you.

MICHAEL: A distinction you never made clear to him I imagine.

ANNE: I did. But perhaps a bit late.

MICHAEL: To have loved Anne Frank, to think she loved you
               back. To find out you were wrong. That could ruin
               a life I imagine.

ANNE: Well imagine away, because you will never know.

               They smile at each other, kiss.

               *MICHAEL leaves. ANNE sits down and begins to
               write, oblivious to all that's around her, as the stage
               becomes the bridal shop. MARGOT appears in a
               wedding dress.*

Scene 6

               In the bridal shop.

MARGOT: What about this one?

ANNE: That's beautiful.

MARGOT: Yes?

ANNE: Of course, they are all lovely.

MARGOT: But is it the one? *(No response from ANNE.)* Anne?

ANNE: Yes?

MARGOT: Do you think this is the one?

ANNE: I don't know Margot. They all look so much alike.
               To be honest, I can't tell this one from the last.

MARGOT: I wish you wouldn't be this way.

ANNE: What way?

MARGOT: Acting as though this is all somehow beneath you.

ANNE: I'm not.

MARGOT: You are.

ANNE: I'm not. I'm just not as interested in these sorts of things. You should have brought Mother.

MARGOT: Are you sure that's it?

ANNE: What do you mean?

MARGOT: I understand if maybe this is a little hard for you.

ANNE: What?

MARGOT: I'm getting married, moving on with my life. I understand if you might be feeling a bit…

ANNE: A bit…?

MARGOT: Well, a bit jealous. But it is completely understandable!

ANNE laughs.

Is that funny?

ANNE: Jealous because you're getting married? Oh Margot. I don't care about that sort of thing. You know that.

MARGOT: I know you always say that but—

ANNE: No, no—you mustn't worry about me being jealous of you. That's silly.

MARGOT: Oh.

MARGOT gets up and further fiddles with her dress, obviously hurt.

ANNE: I didn't mean…I just mean—

MARGOT: Well perhaps you could put that scribbling away for five minutes and pay attention to what's going on in the room. For goodness sakes, I wish at least you'd pretend that the people in your life are as important as the characters in your book.

ANNE, after a moment of shock, puts away her notebook, ashamed. She approaches MARGOT. ANNE picks up a gorgeous long veil. She places the veil on MARGOT's head as they look in the mirror.

ANNE: Oh my. Look at you! You must get this one.

MARGOT: I don't know.

ANNE: It's beautiful.

MARGOT: I feel silly in all this. Perhaps I am too old to be making such a big deal.

ANNE: Too old? Margot.

MARGOT: Well I'm no blushing bride. *(Whispering.)* I am almost thirty.

ANNE: So what? You're beautiful. *(Beat.)* And you simply must have this veil! It makes you look like a real bride!

MARGOT: I don't even know if I can afford it.

ANNE: You don't have to. It's my gift to you.

MARGOT: Don't be ridiculous.

ANNE: Don't you be. I'm a working girl now.

MARGOT: Thank you.

MARGOT begins to change back into her dress.

ANNE: Margot.

MARGOT: Yes?

ANNE: Never mind. Well, I was just thinking…

MARGOT:	Out with it!
ANNE:	Perhaps I can bring a guest to the wedding?
MARGOT:	Of course. Of course you can.
ANNE:	I wasn't going to. But—
MARGOT:	I insist.
ANNE:	Alright then.
MARGOT:	This is the mystery man you've been hiding from us for months?
ANNE:	What?
MARGOT:	Oh, come now. I might not be as clever as you, but I am no fool.
ANNE:	Yes. It's been some time that we've been seeing each other.
MARGOT:	Well. Wonderful then. I look forward to meeting him.
ANNE:	Margot. You know him.
MARGOT:	What do you mean?
ANNE:	It's Michael Stein.

A pause. MARGOT is shocked. She has gone pale, maybe a bit faint. She tries her best to hold it together.

MARGOT:	Michael?
ANNE:	I'm sorry I kept it a secret. I just didn't want things to get complicated.

MARGOT says nothing.

What is it? What's the matter?

MARGOT: Is that what you've been doing all this time? I get
            you a job and this is how you behave?

ANNE: What? No. Not at all. One thing has nothing to do
            with the other.

MARGOT: I see.

            MARGOT begins to get out of the wedding dress.

ANNE: Are you—Margot, are you jealous?

MARGOT: Don't be ridiculous. I'm getting married. I wouldn't
            want to be embroiled in some fling with a man old
            enough to be my father.

ANNE: He's not that old—

MARGOT: Another one Anne. I can't believe it.

ANNE: What are you talking about?

MARGOT: All of that time I answered his phone and took his
            memos. He never even noticed I was breathing.

ANNE: That's not true! He adored you. He is disappointed
            in me on a daily basis thanks to you, believe me.

MARGOT: That's not what I'm talking about.

ANNE: But. You have no feelings for Michael do you? You
            love George.

MARGOT: Of course.

ANNE: I mean, you never even mentioned Michael in that
            way all the time you were working there…

MARGOT: Well of course not, I wouldn't.

ANNE: What do you mean?

MARGOT: You just…you really don't know do you? You
            are just so oblivious. You never think of another

person. You can't see past the nose on your face. It's just like the attic.

ANNE: The attic?

MARGOT: I was there too! But I didn't stand a chance. You set your eyes on Peter and didn't give it a second thought.

ANNE: Didn't give what a second thought?

MARGOT: That I might have liked him? That I was eighteen years old and could have done with some male attention myself? It never even occurred to you that I might be interested in him, that he might be interested in me! The world has to revolve around Anne Frank.

ANNE: But what does it have to do with—

MARGOT: —I remember, I remember, Anne! I remember that we all have to play your game. And nothing ever changes with you, does it?

ANNE: Margot, I'm…I'm sorry.

MARGOT: I wish him luck, Mr. Stein. Poor fellow. Doesn't know what he's gotten himself into.

ANNE: Well, I think he's beginning to figure it out.

A moment. They look at each other. MARGOT is suddenly shocked by her own outburst.

MARGOT: Oh, Anne. I'm sorry!

ANNE: No, you're right. I should have asked you. He was your friend first.

MARGOT: No, no! I just want you to be happy. I don't know what came over me. I'm…I'm so nervous.

She begins to get teary eyed.

ANNE: Oh Margot.

MARGOT: It seems too good to be true. There were times when I wasn't sure we would even…

ANNE: I know.

MARGOT: None of this would have been. No George, no wedding…it's like I am standing on the edge of a cliff, and if I think about it too much, about all the others who didn't…it's like I can fall over the edge just from the thought of it.

ANNE: Margot.

MARGOT: It's alright. I just have to let those thoughts go when they come. Just let them in and out by focusing on one thing. This floor. This mirror. My ring. It's real. And it's in front of me now.

MARGOT looks in the mirror, and at ANNE behind her.

ANNE: You'll be beautiful.

MARGOT smiles and begins to change back into her clothes. ANNE stands around, trying to be attentive, but she steals sidelong glances at her notebook.

Do you mind if I just…?

MARGOT: Oh, alright then, go ahead. I know you're dying to write something down.

ANNE: It's just—you've inspired me! The Martha character…what if she left behind a fiancé when they went into hiding? I just want to make sure I write it down before I forget it.

MARGOT: Well go ahead. I wouldn't want to be the one to doom poor Martha to a life of spinsterhood.

> *ANNE hurries to jot something down.*
>
> *(Suddenly realizing.)* Anne, have you told Peter about Michael?

ANNE: Not yet.

MARGOT: You know Peter hasn't proposed yet.

ANNE: I know.

MARGOT: It's been months since he bought that ring. He's just been carrying it around with him. Waiting...

ANNE: Waiting for what?

MARGOT: I don't know. *(MARGOT looks at ANNE.)* A sign perhaps.

ANNE: *(Pause.)* Peter is an adult. He has to make his own choices. *(Pause.)* Alright. I'll tell him.

MARGOT: When?

ANNE: Soon. Before the wedding.

MARGOT: Good.

> *MARGOT is changed now. The sisters look at each other.*

ANNE: So?

MARGOT: So?

ANNE: Do you want the shoes as well?

MARGOT: Oh Anne. *(Beat.)* Of course I want the shoes.

> *The girls giggle.*
>
> *MARGOT gathers her wedding items and leaves. ANNE sits back down to finish the thought she was writing about. MICHAEL appears on stage, waits*

*for a moment, impatiently, then hustles her into her
coat. They walk for a bit as the stage becomes outside
in Brooklyn. PETER appears, sees them, but hides
off in the shadows.*

Scene 7

On the street outside ANNE's apartment.

ANNE: Well you've walked me home, you've done your
                duty. Good night.

MICHAEL: Why are you cross?

ANNE: I am not cross, I'm merely tired. *(Fakes a yawn.)* Off
                to bed with me. Goodnight.

MICHAEL: Just because I disagreed with you.

ANNE: Dismissed. You dismissed me.

MICHAEL: Well I'm sorry, but what you said was ridiculous!

ANNE: Why? I'm entitled to my opinions.

MICHAEL: Gregory Peck? A bore?

ANNE: That is right.

MICHAEL: *(Amused.)* Oh come on. You can't be serious.

ANNE: I am serious.

MICHAEL: You'll say anything to be contrarian.

ANNE: No I won't!

MICHAEL: Just because everyone else loves him, you can't.

ANNE: No, that's not it. I simply don't understand all the
                hubbub.

MICHAEL: You don't think he's handsome?

ANNE: Well of course he's handsome. But that doesn't make someone interesting does it?

MICHAEL: Doesn't it?

ANNE: A person can be beautiful and uninteresting don't you think? I mean...well what about Audrey Hepburn?

MICHAEL: Hard to tell, she's so grotesque.

ANNE: *(Laughing.)* Oh, alright.

MICHAEL: No I really find her repulsive. I had to shield my eyes when she was on the screen.

ANNE: You are going to leave me for Audrey Hepburn aren't you?

MICHAEL: *(As if to put her at ease.)* Anne, if Audrey Hepburn herself made the offer... *(Thinking better of it.)* then quite possibly, yes.

ANNE: Well I suppose I can't argue with that. It's agreed then. Audrey Hepburn it is.

MICHAEL: Thank you Miss Frank.

ANNE: A pleasure doing business with you Mr. Stein.

They kiss. Unable to pretend anymore, PETER emerges from the shadows.

PETER: Anne?

ANNE pulls away from MICHAEL.

ANNE: Peter! What a surprise! What are you doing here?

PETER: I've come to see you. You haven't been answering the phone much.

ANNE: Well, I've been out.

PETER: Yes, it seems you are always out.

ANNE: We were seeing a movie. *Roman Holiday*. Have you seen it?

PETER: No. Shall I?

ANNE: Oh yes, it's quite good.

PETER: Wonderful.

           Pause.

MICHAEL: Michael Stein.

PETER: Peter van Pels.

ANNE: Oh goodness, I'm sorry, of course.

MICHAEL: Pleasure to meet you van Pels. I've heard a lot about you.

PETER: Oh yes? Well I wish I could say the same.

           Pause.

           Anne, do you have a moment?

ANNE: Of course. Why don't we all go upstairs for a spot of coffee?

PETER: No I'd rather not.

ANNE: Don't be silly it's cold out.

PETER: I like it.

ANNE: But Peter—

PETER: *(Snapping at her.)* The cold is fine.

ANNE: Fine then. *(Beat.)* Is everything alright?

PETER: No, not really.

           He looks at MICHAEL, who has lit a cigarette.

MICHAEL: Cigarette?

PETER: No thank you.

MICHAEL: *(Opening his pack.)* Good thing because it looks like
                I'm out anyway. *(Pause.)* Maybe I'll just duck away
                and get another pack.

ANNE: That's fine dear. I am home now. Peter can make
                sure I get in alright.

MICHAEL: All right doll. See you tomorrow.

                He goes to kiss her and she offers her cheek.

                Nice to meet you Peter. Take care of our girl.

                *He slaps PETER's arm, maybe a bit too hard, as he
                exits.*

ANNE: What is it Peter? What's the matter?

PETER: Who is that?

ANNE: That's Michael.

PETER: Michael?

ANNE: Yes, from my office.

PETER: Your boss? Does he always walk you home?

ANNE: No, I told you we've been to a movie.

PETER: Yes, *Roman Holiday.*

ANNE: Yes.

PETER: Of course.

ANNE: Peter van Pels, what on Earth is the matter with
                you?

PETER: I don't know. What is the matter with me? How can
                I be so foolish?

ANNE: What are you talking about?

PETER: Something is wrong, something has happened.

ANNE: *(Suddenly very afraid.)* What is it? Is it your mother? Your father.

PETER: It's Betty.

ANNE: Betty! Oh no! Is she ill?

PETER: No.

ANNE: Has she left you? Or turned down your proposal?

PETER: No, Anne.

ANNE: For God's sake, what then?

PETER: I hate her.

ANNE: *(Stunned.)* What a thing to say.

PETER: It's true.

ANNE: Nonsense. You're going to marry her. You've picked out the ring and everything.

PETER: I've left her.

ANNE: No, no Peter.

PETER: How Anne? How can I marry her when—

ANNE: Well, when we meet the right person—

PETER: The right person? You yourself said it...maybe she's not the right one after all.

ANNE: But, she's a lovely girl. She's bright and beautiful. She comes from a good family. She's perfect for you.

PETER: You never liked her before. *(ANNE says nothing.)* But now you've met someone else. You don't need me hanging about.

ANNE: No Peter, that's not it.

PETER: You said I shouldn't marry someone if I don't love
           her.

ANNE: Maybe you do love her.

PETER: No, I don't.

ANNE: *(Exasperated.)* Well why ever not?

PETER: You know why.

ANNE: You have to give her a chance. She'll get to know
           you. That's what marriage is for.

PETER: Is it?

ANNE: *(Backing away from him.)* Let's go upstairs, and get
           out of the cold.

PETER: What about us Anne?

ANNE: Peter, Michael and I—

PETER: Michael? Who is he? Who is Betty for that matter?
           They're no one. Strangers to us. You've been my
           whole world since I was sixteen years old. I bought
           this for you. *(He pulls out the ring.)* And when we
           kissed, I knew it for sure—

ANNE: Peter, no! No. I can't. In so many ways you have
           my heart. You always will. But…it isn't…that way.
           It just isn't.

PETER: Oh. So that's it then?

ANNE: I'm sorry.

PETER: *(Pause.)* Do you love him?

ANNE: Can we please go upstairs?

PETER: Is it love, Anne?

           Pause.

ANNE: Yes.

PETER: Oh. Then it's just me. It's just me you can't love.

ANNE: Peter, you are going to get married and forget all
                   about me.

PETER: I suppose. I suppose I am. What else am I to do?

                   *He leaves. She looks after him as VIRGINIA
                   enters.*

ANNE: *(Calling after him.)* Peter. Peter!

VIRGINIA: Miss Frank.

ANNE: Yes?

Scene 8

                   VIRGINIA's office.

VIRGINIA: Hello again.

ANNE: Miss Belair. You're looking well.

VIRGINIA: I'm old and single, but I'm rich, so I guess I can't
                   complain, right?

ANNE: No, I suppose not.

VIRIGINIA: And you? How is the big city treating our little
                   German girl?

ANNE: Uh—fine. Just fine. I am working, and writing. I am
                   writing all the time.

VIRGINIA: I can see that.

ANNE: I am very excited about the new turn the story has
                   taken.

VIRGINIA: Uh-huh. And tell me about your life. You have a
                   fella?

ANNE: A fella?

VIRIGINIA: Sure, pretty little thing like you. You must be in the market. What about that old boyfriend of yours, Pierre?

ANNE: He's Pierre in the book. His real name is Peter.

VIRIGINIA: Of course.

ANNE: No. He's, well…engaged.

VIRGINIA: Oh?

ANNE: To someone else.

VIRGINIA: I gathered. I thought maybe since this book ended differently than the memoir, you had a different ending too.

ANNE: Well you were saying that losing interest in the relationship wasn't as romantic, would be harder to sell…

VIRGINIA: Did I?

ANNE: Yes, don't you remember?

VIRGINIA: Sure, sure. Sounds like something I would say. Well, too bad. It's nice to have a beau. Maybe even a husband.

ANNE: You don't.

VIRGINIA: (Laughs.) No cherish. Never had the pleasure. Well, never had the time to be honest. But you're young. Still lots of time for children, a house, you know the American dream.

ANNE: I'm sorry, have you brought me here to talk about my book, or my love life?

VIRGINIA: Alright kitten. You're impatient, I get it. I'm making a point here.

ANNE: And that is?

VIRIGINIA: The book…it's not going to happen.

ANNE: What? Why not?

VIRIGINIA: Look babydoll, I tried to tell you last time, the story is problematic.

ANNE: But I've changed it so much. It's not even true anymore.

VIRGINIA: And to be honest, it doesn't feel true.

ANNE: What?

VIRIGINIA: Well at least as a memoir, it had the ring of authenticity. There was something intriguing about the fact that we knew it happened. Now that it's just fiction, it loses some of that cachet.

ANNE: I see.

VIRGINIA: And, if we're getting really honest, the writing is immature. It feels like it was written by a kid.

ANNE: It's about me when…it's about a fourteen year old.

               VIRGINIA, starting to lose her patience, fishes a cigarette out and lights it.

VIRGINIA: And it feels like it was written by one. No, this isn't going to work. All this talk of God and survival—

ANNE: It's dramatic.

VIRGINIA: No, it isn't. Nothing happens.

ANNE: Nothing on the outside happens, but this is because they are waiting. They are stuck, you see? But— there is so much inner life— *(She begins to pull out her papers and notes, and she pulls Kitty out.)*

VIRGINIA:	Is that your diary? The same one? There's your problem sister. It's the source material. Why are you working from that same old journal?
ANNE:	Kitty?
VIRGINIA:	It has a name?

ANNE just looks at her.

It's an albatross.

ANNE:	Pardon?
VIRGINIA:	You've got to get rid of it. Start new.
ANNE:	I could never get rid of Kitty.
VIRGINIA:	It's just some pages. It's not a person.
ANNE:	But the novel—
VIRGINIA:	Is not happening. You should forget it.
ANNE:	But...but you told me to expand the story, to give it more humour, more twists and turns. I did what you said.
VIRGINIA:	In a manner of speaking—
ANNE:	I can't understand why you are rejecting me again.
VIRGINIA:	Listen sister, this thing is not an exact science. It's not as simple as plugging some numbers into a formula. If it was, everyone would do it.
ANNE:	*(Looking ill.)* I've just spent six months writing it.
VIRIGINIA:	And you're getting good! You're a good writer. Your English is a lot better this time around. But you're still young, you're still working in a new language, you're still working with a flawed story. It's time to move on.

ANNE: This is my story. My version of the most significant thing to happen in modern times.

VIRGINIA: Look Miss Frank. I don't mean to upset you... again. I'm just saying, this is all rather fresh for you. And I get the feeling that you might just be too close to it to have any perspective. Catch yourself a nice husband, settle down, pop out a few brats and you'll see. The world is a whole lot bigger than some attic in Amsterdam.

               VIRGINIA hands ANNE back her manuscript.

               VIRGINIA exits. ANNE, now carrying the diary, and the manuscript for both the memoir and the novel, is unsure what to do with them. She puts down the pile of pages on a table as she takes off her clothes and is left in her slip. A bed appears onstage as the scene moves to MICHAEL's apartment. She moves the manuscript and Kitty to the foot of the bed where she finds a wedding dress. She holds it up to her, see if she likes it on. MICHAEL comes on in his undergarments, sees her. He puts his arms around her from behind and they dance for a bit. She grows distracted, lets the wedding dress fall to the ground.

Scene 9

               ANNE and MICHAEL, just married. Drunk.

MICHAEL: Well. I was beginning to wonder if you would go through with it.

ANNE: Don't be silly.

MICHAEL: Three postponements. I don't think that's normal.

ANNE: Well it's done now isn't it?

MICHAEL: That it is.

ANNE: Do you suppose things will be very different now?

MICHAEL: Probably. Things are always different.

ANNE: You mean when you get married?

MICHAEL: I mean all the time.

ANNE: Mr. Stein. Are you drunk?

MICHAEL: No. Yes. But not drunk enough.

ANNE: Not too drunk now! I need you to have control of all your faculties.

MICHAEL: Oh dear. Rest my love! I need rest! Don't forget I am much older than you are.

ANNE: Hogwash. *(Rising, realizing she is drunk.)* Oh my. Perhaps rest is in order. *(She sees her wedding dress and picks it up off the floor.)* What can I do with this thing now?

MICHAEL: Hold onto it. You might need it again. *(She looks at him.)* I'm not going to live forever you know.

ANNE: Oh Michael. What a thing to say. I could never marry again. Not in the same dress! *(They laugh.)* What a ridiculous thing. A wedding dress. What a ridiculous thing. A wedding.

MICHAEL: Too late to question it now.

ANNE: *(Considering the dress.)* I suppose I could dye it a different colour. Wear it to something else. *(Pause.)* I suppose I shouldn't have worn white.

MICHAEL: I won't tell anyone if you don't.

ANNE: Tell me something Mr. Stein.

MICHAEL: Yes, Mrs. Stein?

ANNE: Oh dear. That will take some getting used to.

MICHAEL: What my dear Anne?

ANNE: Tell me, do you think of other women?

MICHAEL: Who has time?

ANNE: Come on. You must think of other women once in a while. After all, you've had so many women in your time.

MICHAEL: Why on earth would you want to talk about this?

ANNE: It excites me.

MICHAEL: It excites you? Oh my.

ANNE: Come now. You know all my secrets.

MICHAEL: Well, you wrote a book about them.

ANNE: So what about you?

MICHAEL: You're the one with the imagination, you tell me.

ANNE: I picture you dancing through a room of women, tall, gorgeous... New Yorkers! Beautiful American women who want you, who are vying for your attention. You spin then and dip them but always move on, always keep looking. Then you come to me. A small, Semitic, European mouse of a girl... Someone most people wouldn't even notice. And there you stop. For good. You choose me.

MICHAEL: I do. (*He starts kissing her.*)

ANNE: Why?

MICHAEL: Why what?

ANNE: Why did you choose me?

MICHAEL: You know.

ANNE: *(She pushes him away a bit.)* No I don't. Out of all the sophisticated, beautiful women—

MICHAEL: Oh Anne.

ANNE: No really. Why me?

MICHAEL: It must be your shy, retiring nature.

ANNE: Answer the question.

MICHAEL: The deed is done. The answer matters not.

ANNE: You will answer.

MICHAEL: Or what?

ANNE: Or your young wife will withhold her feminine wiles for as long as it takes.

MICHAEL: You wouldn't.

ANNE: No?

MICHAEL: You couldn't.

ANNE: I lived in an attic for three years. Are you willing to find out just how far my self-discipline can go?

         They stare at each other. Stalemate.

MICHAEL: *(He pulls away from her. Sits up. Thinks.)* Did I have my fair share of women? Yes. Were there offers along the way? Sure. But I never took them seriously because I didn't really know what I wanted until I met you. I chose you, Anne, because you know who you are, and who you want to be. You are a new kind of woman. Don't tell me I was wrong.

         Pause. ANNE takes this in. He goes to kiss her and she pulls away.

ANNE: It's too quiet in here. How about some music?

         ANNE goes to the record player and pulls out

a record. MICHAEL goes to get the bottle of champagne to her to pour her another one.

MICHAEL: Something new?

ANNE: Just came out.

MICHAEL: You'll put me in the poor house.

ANNE: But we'll have fun getting there. Maybe it's time for another drink.

MICHAEL: *(Handing her a glass.)* I've never seen you enjoy alcohol quite so much.

ANNE: On occasion.

             ANNE drops the needle on the record, and "I Put a Spell on You" by Screaming J. Hawkins comes on.

MICHAEL: You've been drinking all night.

ANNE: All day.

MICHAEL: Since before the wedding? *(He hands her a glass.)*

ANNE: It gives me courage. *(She drinks fast.)*

MICHAEL: Courage?

ANNE: *(Extends her glass for a refill.)* A toast my love.

MICHAEL: *(He fills her glass.)* To my wife.

ANNE: To my husband. To the future.

             ANNE clinks her glass with MICHAEL.

MICHAEL: *L'chaim.*

ANNE: *L'chaim.*

             They drink. Kiss.

The song rises and swells. MICHAEL collapses back on the bed. A spotlight hits ANNE as she looks down at Kitty, at the foot of the bed.

Blackout.

Act II

Scene 9

1962.

ANNE, MICHAEL, MARGOT and PETER are on stage in their winter coats. PETER stands away. He wears a black armband. The sound of the Mourners' Kaddish begins. ANNE looks at PETER. PETER exits, as do MARGOT and MICHAEL. ANNE takes off her coat and begins to wander around the room, which is PETER's study.

Scene 10

PETER's study in Toronto. PETER enters. He sees ANNE, already there.

ANNE: Hello.

PETER: Anne. Hello.

ANNE: I was looking for a telephone, I—

PETER: Yes there's one here.

ANNE: That's all right. I don't need it.

PETER: Oh.

ANNE: *(Pause.)* Peter, I'm so sorry—

PETER: Yes, well. Thank you.

ANNE:	I hope it's OK that we're here.
PETER:	Of course. It's good to see you.
ANNE:	And you. It's been such a long time. Years. *(Pause. They stand far apart.)* It's my first time in Canada. I'd like to see some polar bears!
PETER:	Well, those are quite far away I'm afraid.
ANNE:	Yes, that is what Michael said. He warned I might be disappointed in Toronto. It always seemed such a far off exotic place.
PETER:	Hardly.
ANNE:	Well compared to Brooklyn anyway.
PETER:	Oh. Well. Compared to Brooklyn.

PETER goes to pour himself a drink of something strong.

ANNE:	It's amazing how common a place becomes so quickly. I dreamed of New York as a child. The buildings, the people. And now, it's just another place to live. Magic doesn't last I suppose. *(PETER says nothing.)* Where are the polar bears then?
PETER:	In Manitoba. Northern Manitoba. Near the Arctic.
ANNE:	The Arctic! Imagine that. You live in the same country as the Arctic.
PETER:	Yes, well. It doesn't affect me much on the day to day.
ANNE:	No, I suppose it wouldn't. *(Pause.)* Peter, I'm so sorry about Gusti. It had been years since I had seen her. Not since Margot's wedding. She seemed so alive then.
PETER:	It had already started, we just didn't know it.

ANNE: (*Pause.*) Well. I've been trying to think about her. Playing "I remember" all about Gusti. To recall what she was like. But for some reason, it seems like all I can remember now is the way I spoke to her in the attic. I've had many conversations with her since, but somehow it's as if none of that ever happened. (*Pause.*) I said so many careless things to her when we were in hiding. Things I wish I'd never said. I hope...I hope I didn't hurt her.

PETER: She was fond of you.

ANNE: Was she?

PETER: Yes.

ANNE: That's such a relief. I can't begin to tell you...the things I've said to people...it keeps me up at night. But I suppose when you talk as much as I do, you are bound to end up saying things you regret.

PETER: I usually regret the things I don't say.

ANNE: Well I suppose there's no getting it right is there?

PETER: No, not really.

          Pause.

ANNE: Your home is lovely.

PETER: Thank you.

ANNE: It's so nice to finally see it. To look and say, "Here's where Peter eats. Here's where he talks on the telephone." I've pictured it so many times. (*Pause.*) Betty has such immaculate taste. And the boys are so—

PETER: Yes.

ANNE: I am sure they brought much comfort to your mother at the end.

PETER: No, not really.

ANNE: Oh.

PETER: She didn't know who any of us were. She was
            always trying to take her clothes off. They hadn't
            seen her in months. We had to put her into a mental
            hospital. Not an appropriate place for children.

ANNE: (Pause.) I don't know what to say.

PETER: (Pause.) There's nothing to say.

ANNE: I've missed you so.

            PETER says nothing.

ANNE: Are you still angry with me? After all these years?
            For things that I did and said when I was a girl?
            Hardly more than a child? Don't you know I
            would never... All I have ever hoped for was your
            happiness.

PETER: Happiness is a luxury of women.

ANNE: Is that right?

PETER: Yes. Men don't have time to think of happiness.
            We have to marry and provide. We have to earn
            everything. We have to settle for what we get. And
            very few of us get what we want. Even fewer of us
            are happy. We just manage to get on with it.

ANNE: That's not true.

PETER: I know it doesn't suit you. But that's the way it is.

ANNE: Michael seems happy.

PETER: Yes. He does, doesn't he?

            They look at each other.

ANNE: What good was it all then? What good was it all if
            you aren't even happy?

PETER: What good indeed? What good is it all if you just come to the end of your life and forget your children? Your grandchildren? If you don't even recognize your own face in the mirror? If you think your clothes are on fire and that your caretakers are trying to kill you? If you wake up day in and day out and think you are still up there, still in the attic, still afraid that every footstep is the Nazis outside your door?

ANNE: She didn't.

PETER: You tell me, what good is any of it?

ANNE: Perhaps it's not then. But here we are.

PETER: Here we are.

            She cries. Regretting his tone, he goes to comfort her. He takes her in his arms. They look at each other. She kisses him. He pulls away.

ANNE: I'm sorry.

PETER: Why did you do that?

ANNE: I don't know.

PETER: You've always been cruel.

ANNE: No, you just looked so sad.

            Beat.

PETER: Anne. Why did you do it?

ANNE: I didn't mean to. It just happened.

PETER: No not that. Why did you make me fall in love with you?

ANNE: What?

PETER: In the attic.

ANNE: Oh Peter, please. I'm no magician. I can't make anyone fall in love with me.

PETER: But you did. You pursued me with singular purpose and you made me fall in love with you.

ANNE: Don't be silly.

PETER: It's true.

ANNE: It's not!

PETER: Then why do I love you so? *(Pause.)* I want to know why. I think you owe me that.

ANNE: *(Pause.)* I was lonely.

PETER: And?

ANNE: And…and that's it.

PETER: No. It isn't.

ANNE: I was frightened.

PETER: And?

ANNE: What do you want from me?

PETER: I want the truth.

ANNE: Peter!

PETER: Say it Anne. I want you to say it.

ANNE: And! And I wanted to see…to see if I could do it.

PETER: Yes. That's it.

ANNE: I was young. A child. I didn't know that it would have…such a profound effect on you.

PETER: No of course not. It was you and your diary. And whatever it took to fill those pages, that's what you would do.

ANNE: Is that what you think? How can you—

PETER: What I don't understand is why you couldn't love
               me back?

               ANNE looks at him. Pause.

ANNE: I did—

PETER: Not the way I wanted.

ANNE: No, perhaps not that way. But I did. And I do. I miss
               you terribly, you know.

PETER: So you've said.

ANNE: And it's true. Why don't you believe me?

PETER: I believe you. Why wouldn't I?

ANNE: But you never return my calls or letters, not in five
               years.

PETER: Not everything is about what you need. There's
               nothing to be done.

               Beat.

ANNE: How is Betty?

PETER: Betty is…wonderful. She deserves far better than
               me.

ANNE: No, don't say that. You're a wonderful boy. Man.

PETER: I might have been. When you knew me. I'm not the
               person I was.

               Pause.

ANNE: Remember the attic?

PETER: Of course I do.

ANNE: It was awful wasn't it?

PETER: Yes.

ANNE: I want to tell people about it. About how we survived. About how we all turned out.

PETER: I know you do, darling.

ANNE: But it's different now. Before, before it was because I wanted people to notice me. But now I worry, as time passes...they'll never notice Gusti, and the way she made your father light up. They'll never know about Miep, how she risked everything. No one will know what a wonderful boy you were. How you saved me.

           She touches him. After a moment, he gently removes her hand from him and steps away.

PETER: There are millions of stories the world will never know.

ANNE: Peter. I don't know what I should do.

PETER: You should...have a good life.

ANNE: Don't say that. That's something you say to someone you'll never speak to again.

PETER: No. I'm just saying. It's what you should do. Have a good life.

ANNE: How?

PETER: I have no idea.

           They stand in silence.

           There is a gentle groan from off stage. ANNE turns to see where its come from. MARGOT steps on stage. She is about eight months pregnant and out of breath. She pauses for a moment. ANNE turns back to see PETER, but he's left. She rushes to help MARGOT.

Scene 11

> *MARGOT's apartment. ANNE helps her into the chair.*

ANNE: What is it? Is it time?

MARGOT: No, no. He's just shifting about.

> *ANNE tidies up around the apartment. Ties herself into an apron and picks up a cleaning rag.*

He's heavier than Miep was at this point.

ANNE: He just seems that way because he's the second. And you're four years older.

MARGOT: Don't remind me.

ANNE: You keep calling him "he". Are you so sure it's a boy?

MARGOT: I hope so. The way he's always squirming. With that much urge to move about, he's likely to be a boy.

ANNE: Or an unfortunate girl, like her Auntie.

MARGOT: Heaven forbid.

> *ANNE playfully hits her with a dishtowel in her hand.*

And what about you?

ANNE: What about me?

MARGOT: Aren't you ready yet?

ANNE: Well we're trying.

MARGOT: Are you?

ANNE: Yes. Almost a year now.

MARGOT: Really. And no luck?

ANNE: I guess it's just not the right time yet. I nearly forgot! I've brought a record.

MARGOT: Did you? A new one?

ANNE: You'll love it!

ANNE puts on "Mama Said" by the Shirelles. She dances and sings along for a moment.

Dance with me!

MARGOT: Anne! I can't possibly!

ANNE pulls MARGOT out of her chair and they dance for a bit. MARGOT tries to keep up, but can't.

(Laughing.) Oh my goodness! I think that's enough!

ANNE: It's good for you to keep active!

MARGOT: Unless you want me to have this baby on the floor here, turn it off!

ANNE: Alright!

MARGOT sits. ANNE turns off the music.

MARGOT: Thanks for keeping me company.

ANNE: My pleasure.

MARGOT: I don't know. I wasn't nearly as nervous with Miep.

ANNE: Of course you were.

MARGOT: I don't remember being.

ANNE: Well you've forgotten because it makes it easier to have another.

MARGOT: Says who?

ANNE: Says me.

MARGOT: But where did you hear it?

ANNE: I just made it up.

MARGOT: Did you now?

ANNE: Yes. But I think it sounds quite good, don't you?

MARGOT: Quite good indeed.

ANNE: Have you chosen a name?

MARGOT: A more accurate question is have we agreed upon a name?

ANNE: Oh dear.

MARGOT: Hmph.

ANNE: So?

MARGOT: Well I like Victor or Jan—

ANNE: But?

MARGOT: But George insists that in America, Jan is a girl's name.

ANNE: A girl's name?

MARGOT: The way it is spelled.

ANNE: And Victor?

MARGOT: Too German.

ANNE: So what does he want to call him?

MARGOT: Norman.

ANNE: Norman!

MARGOT: Isn't that dreadful?

ANNE: Why Norman?

MARGOT: It was his uncle's name. But no one even liked the man. And he said there's some painter or someone, as if that would convince me. I hate it.

ANNE: Oh dear. Perhaps you should be praying for a girl.

MARGOT: I know. But George is just desperate for a boy to play catch and go to ball games with.

ANNE: Americans and their baseball. *(She stops.)* What will you call her, if she's a girl?

MARGOT: Auguste.

ANNE: Margot. That's lovely.

MARGOT: Yes, I think Peter will be pleased.

ANNE: Have you asked him?

MARGOT: No.

ANNE: But you've spoken?

MARGOT: Anne.

ANNE: I know. I'm not supposed to ask.

ANNE goes about, dusting things, and tidying.

MARGOT: Why torture yourself?

ANNE: I just…miss him.

MARGOT: The pair of you were too…involved. Too wrapped up in each other. Some distance will do you good. Say, did you bring me anything to read?

ANNE: Not today.

MARGOT: Why not?

ANNE: Nothing new.

MARGOT: Nothing new? Well, read me an old one.

ANNE: An old one? Margot Katz, it's not like you to indulge in anything old.

MARGOT: Well maybe revisiting an old story will get the blood pumping again. Get you back on track.

ANNE looks at her.

ANNE: Michael told you didn't he?

MARGOT: Now Anne—

ANNE: Damn him, I told him not to say anything.

MARGOT: He's worried. He's worried about you.

ANNE: So he needed to worry you? You don't have enough on your mind?

MARGOT: I never have too much on my mind to leave you out of it.

ANNE: Oh Margot.

MARGOT: What is it then?

ANNE: I just can't.

MARGOT: Perhaps this is a sign. That you should get on with your life

ANNE: What do you mean? Writing is my life.

MARGOT: It's time to get on with the rest of it. With real life.

ANNE: Real life.

MARGOT: Yes of course. *(Pause.)* Well this is not a life.

ANNE: What does that mean?

MARGOT: Don't you want a family?

ANNE: Of course I do. I told you, we're trying.

MARGOT: Really? Why are you on birth control then?

ANNE: *(Shocked.)* Excuse me?

MARGOT: Dr. Kaplan suggested I try it, once the baby is here.
             He said it's a good way of timing if and when we
             want our next baby. He said my sister was very
             happy with her experience.

ANNE: I can't believe he told you that. He had no right, no
             right at all!

MARGOT: You're right he didn't. It's none of my business. But
             you're lying to me, to Michael. What do you think
             will come of this?

ANNE: I just need a little more time. I need my whole heart
             and mind in this…otherwise, to come this far and
             give up? When *The Secret Annex* gets published
             then I can begin to—

MARGOT: And what if it doesn't get published?

ANNE: What do you mean?

MARGOT: It might not.

ANNE: Why are you saying that?

MARGOT: Because I think you need to face the truth.

ANNE: But don't you think it's good?

MARGOT: What I think doesn't matter. What you think
             doesn't matter. Don't you see? Wanting and hoping
             and wishing will not make it happen.

ANNE: I know that! I'm just not ready to put my life aside
             to take care of children. Some day—

MARGOT: What day? You're not getting younger.

ANNE: Margot.

MARGOT: You've been married five years.

ANNE: And I'm still me! Everyone expects me to surrender all my dreams and wants because of a gold band around my finger. Even I expected me to do it. And for a while I tried. I did try. But it's not enough.

MARGOT: Then don't! Don't have children Anne. No one is saying you have to. But for god's sake, do something. Write something else. Travel somewhere. Climb a mountain. Anything. But no, you're waiting. For ten years I've watched you wait and wait... for what? For someone else to tell you it's OK to go on? Do you know what millions of people would have done to— How can you be so selfish?

ANNE: Selfish? For having dreams? If I were a man—

MARGOT: You're not a man!

               Pause.

ANNE: You remind me of mother.

MARGOT: I don't suppose there is any chance that was meant to be a compliment.

ANNE: She's always tried to stifle me. Saying I talked too much, that I never know my place. I can't understand why she didn't find me charming. Why she didn't love me? Everyone else did.

MARGOT: Maybe she was trying to prepare you.

ANNE: For what?

MARGOT: For this world! For what it's like to be a woman with ambition, with dreams. Maybe she was trying to warn you. Dreams are dangerous. If you are going to pin your whole life, your whole existence on a dream—

ANNE: I'm sorry, but I'm not you! I can't just settle for an ordinary life! *(Pause.)* I didn't mean—

Pause.

Margot, I don't have a choice.

MARGOT: You do Anne. You have a choice. You just can't see it. And I love you. But I cannot watch you stand still any longer. I cannot watch you refuse to live your life.

ANNE: Well then. I won't make you watch.

ANNE gathers her things and exits.

Scene 12

ANNE is in VIRGINIA's office. VIRGINIA enters, surprised to find her there. ANNE is on edge. Something is off.

VIRGINIA: Miss Frank?

ANNE: Hello.

VIRGINIA: What are you doing here?

ANNE: I apologize, Miss Belair. Your secretary was at lunch, so I let myself in. *(Admiring the view.)* You're higher up then the last time I was here.

VIRGINIA: Yes, well that happens around here. If you're lucky.

ANNE: Lucky. Yes.

VIRGINIA: You alright?

ANNE: Of course. I'm fine. Why wouldn't I be?

VIRGINIA: I see. Well what do you know? Miss Frank, long time no see.

ANNE: It's Mrs. Stein now.

VIRGINIA: Yes! Yes I read about that. You married Michael Stein, didn't you? Michael Stein partner at Samson, Cohen and Stein? Sure, I read it in the *Times*. Quite a while ago, isn't that right? A few years anyway.

ANNE: Six.

VIRGINIA: It said he was a Harvard man. Not too shabby. How did you two meet?

ANNE: I was…his receptionist.

VIRGINIA: Interesting. I remember reading about him once… he was quite serious about an actress at one point if I recall. What was her name? Well, it was in all the papers. Before the war.

ANNE: Oh.

VIRGINIA: And then I heard some young Kraut snagged him up but I had no idea. Lucky you. I guess it's all in the timing. That must be keeping you busy then. Married life?

ANNE: Well, yes, but I have been working. Believe me, working, working, working.

VIRGINIA: You don't say?

ANNE: Yes.

VIRGINIA: Well that is great. I always thought you had talent.

ANNE: Thank you so much.

VIRGINIA: So listen, why don't you drop off whatever new stuff you've got and make an appointment with Mabel to see me next month.

ANNE: Yes. Yes, all right. Here you are.

             She drops a pile of manuscripts on her desk and

goes to leave. VIRGINIA picks one up, then quickly another.

VIRGINIA: Mrs. Stein?

ANNE: Yes?

VIRGINIA: Uh, is this what I think it is?

ANNE: What do you mean?

VIRGINIA: *(Reading off the front page.) The Secret Annex. (Picking up another manuscript.) The Secret Annex.*

ANNE: Yes, well that first one is the novel, revised.

VIRGINIA holds up the other.

ANNE: That is a stage play I wrote. Based on the story.

VIRGINIA: *(Picking up a third.)* And this one, *The Secret Annex?*

ANNE: Screenplay.

VIRGINIA: I see.

ANNE: There is also a book of short stories and poetry.

VIRGINIA: Let me guess.

ANNE: *Tales from The Secret Annex. (Pause.)* I quite like the title.

VIRGINIA is unable to hide her shock. ANNE spreads out the many manuscripts on the table for VIRGINIA to see.

I wanted to give you options, different versions to choose from. I know, I know, you said the memoir was no good, and the novel, but I've worked on them, and…well, now there are all these other versions. I wanted to make sure I "covered all the bases."

VIRGINIA: I think that is a safe bet.

ANNE: Is something wrong?

VIRGINIA: Mrs. Stein, what is this?

ANNE: This is my story.

VIRGINIA: Yes but—

ANNE: I have approached it from every angle—

VIRGINIA: I can see that.

ANNE: If you would give it a look—

VIRGINIA: Listen sister, we've already been through this—

ANNE: I know, I know but if you would just look at the new work—

VIRGINIA: New? There's nothing new here! This is the same old boring story you been trying to sell me for years.

ANNE: It's my life's work.

VIRGINIA: Well, time to get a new life.

Pause.

You know there are other publishers.

ANNE: I am aware of that.

VIRGINIA: Maybe you'll have better luck with one of the smaller—

ANNE: I've been everywhere.

VIRGINIA: What?

ANNE: I've been everywhere with it. No one wants it.

VIRGINIA: Oh.

ANNE: I thought…I thought because you were a woman, and seemed encouraging once before…

VIRGINIA:	You're a good writer. Why don't you write something else?
ANNE:	I can't…I can't write.
VIRGINIA:	You mean…
ANNE:	I can't write anymore. I have lost the ability.
VIRGINIA:	How long?
ANNE:	About six months.
VIRGINIA:	Writer's block. It happens to everyone.
ANNE:	No, that's not it. I have ideas, whole stories, as I always have. Characters and plots and circumstances—
VIRGINIA:	Good! So what is the problem?
ANNE:	I can't do anything to the people.
VIRGINIA:	What people?
ANNE:	The characters. I can't hurt them. I can't kill them. I can't break their hearts. I can't even make them cry. I keep starting new stories. About the woman down the street. About the old man at the grocery store. About a child I've never met in a ·different country, on a different planet! But I can only get so far because I can't hurt them. I try to give them cancer. Or a heart attack, but I can't. I try to make them betray each other or divorce or lose their jobs. Even age and grow fragile, but it's just not possible. *(ANNE sits.)* I thought "All right then, I won't write about people. I'll write about animals again. Or teddy bears, like I did when I was young." But even that…I can't separate them from their parents. I can't tear their little fur. I can't bear to make even a toy suffer. It's just gotten to be too much. All those lives in my hands. *(She looks at VIRGINIA.)* I'm not crazy! I know they aren't real, but I still can't hurt

them. I tried to write a story about people who lived forever, but that turned out terribly. They were just waiting and waiting. Like the attic...Yes, it's like being in the attic again. Trapped and powerless. So much to say, no way to say it. There are no stories without suffering. And one is not a writer without stories. And who am I if I am not writer? No one. Absolutely no one.

VIRGINIA: You know, not everyone grows up to be what they wanted to be when they were a kid.

ANNE turns away from her. VIRGINIA thinks about this for a moment. She goes to get some scotch. She pours her a drink. ANNE takes it with shaking hands.

I went to Catholic school when I was a child, you know. Don't tell anyone at the country club. I didn't last long. I was always getting in trouble for one thing or another. But while I was there I heard a whole lot of talk about the Jews. Jews, Jews, Jews. Let you in on a little secret, Catholics are obsessed with Jews. They talk about them, a lot. Nothing good mind you. There was one nun, Sister Mary Agnes, I think she was a fanatic. She would just go on and on about how the Jews killed Jesus. They were at fault for the death of our Lord and so on and so forth. Now, I didn't care all that much. I had never even met a Jew, not until I got to college, and from what I knew they were just...other people, same as the coloured, the Irish, that sort of thing. Sort of different from me, but mostly the same as far as I could tell. Besides, Sister Mary Agnes was an idiot, and you didn't need to be a religious scholar to figure out that much. But still even as a kid, even as indifferent as I was, it bothered me. Because it didn't make any sense, you see? When they weren't talking about how the Jews killed the son of God, they were talking about how God sent his only Son down here to die for our sins. Finally, one day in class I laid it out flat. "Sister Mary Agnes, how can we be mad at the Jews for killing someone who was sent here to die for our own good? And besides, didn't he come back to life anyway?" Well. Bye bye Catholic school *(VIRGINIA finishes her drink.)* They don't like too many questions. You can't look at it all that closely, because when one part doesn't make any sense, then the rest of it doesn't hold any water either, see? It just doesn't hold any water.

> *Pause. She checks in with ANNE to see if this is registering. She's not sure.*

Go home. Put this away. Stop thinking about them. It's too many people to try to bring back to life.

> *VIRGINIA exits.*

Scene 13

> *ANNE and MICHAEL's apartment. There are notes everywhere. It is the middle of the night. She sits and reads pages. Scribbles notes on one sheet, then remembers something and looks at another. Something has come unhinged. MICHAEL enters, clearly roused from sleep.*

MICHAEL: Anne?

ANNE: Shh, shh, shh! *(She thinks for a moment, then writes something down.)*

MICHAEL: It's the middle of the night.

ANNE: Yes, I know that.

MICHAEL: Why didn't you come to bed?

ANNE: I can't sleep.

MICHAEL: Why not?

ANNE: Bad dreams.

MICHAEL: What's going on in here? What's this mess?

ANNE: I am trying something new. I have to stop thinking about things so linearly...

MICHAEL: I can't—

ANNE: Never mind. It's not important. I'm writing again! So go back to sleep.

MICHAEL: You're frightening me.

ANNE: No, no, there's nothing to be frightened of. I've figured it all out now.

MICHAEL: What?

ANNE: I have to forget the passage of time. Forget all that. Nothing has happened, it's all still happening.

MICHAEL: I'm calling Dr. Kaplan.

ANNE: Why, so he can tell you all my secrets?

MICHAEL: Anne...

ANNE: No, admit it. You probably know. You know don't you? About the pills.

MICHAEL: You have the right to your privacy.

ANNE: Oh, how gallant of you! I wasn't sure I was a human being until you granted me permission.

MICHAEL: What do you want from me? I am worried about you! You don't sleep. You talk in riddles. I can see you slipping away, and I don't know what to do. Help me.

               Pause.

ANNE: I've been dreaming about it.

MICHAEL: About the attic?

ANNE: In my dream we've never left. We're still there after all these years. Living out our lives in those four rooms. And then there's footsteps. On the landing. On the stairs. They're coming for us. That's when I wake up.

MICHAEL: It sounds normal to me.

ANNE: But that's what I mean. It's not over, Michael. Sometimes I think, what if this part were the dream? What if all of this was the imagined part, and we are still there? We are going to wake up and still be there in the attic. Still waiting for the footsteps.

MICHAEL: (Pause.) They're tearing it down.

ANNE: What?

MICHAEL: Prinsengracht. They're tearing it down. Your father called. Some developer bought the old building. I wasn't going to tell you, I thought it would upset you. But maybe, if it's haunting you so much, maybe it's better you know. It's just an empty old building going to the rats.

ANNE: So that's it then. It will be like it never happened. Except for in my dreams. No one will ever know.

MICHAEL: We'll know it happened. I'll know.

ANNE: But, you're only one person.

MICHAEL: What do you want Anne?

ANNE: I want to know that it matters. That God had a plan, that those years in the annex—

MICHAEL: The annex, the annex! You'd think that is the only thing that's happened to you in your whole life.

ANNE: It might be. In some ways.

MICHAEL: What about us? You and me? Our marriage.

ANNE: Yes, of course that is something too. Of course it is. But it's not special. *(He looks at her.)* Oh Michael, please, please don't take this the wrong way.

MICHAEL: No, how could I take that the wrong way?

ANNE: Marrying you was something so important to me—

MICHAEL: But not special.

ANNE: A lot of people have that experience. It is not a unique experience. I spent three years in that attic under threat of death. I was up there—wondering, dreaming, terrified…alive. How can I expect you to understand? No one understands except Peter.

MICHAEL: Oh, for god's sake.

ANNE: I'm sorry but Peter and I, our relationship—

MICHAEL: What relationship? He wants nothing to do with you! Don't you see that?

ANNE: Of course I see it.

MICHAEL: Then why? Why?

ANNE: Because! He reminds me. Why I'm special.

MICHAEL: He's in love with someone who hasn't existed in fifteen years. I know you, I love you. I think you're special!

ANNE: Do you? Or was it just good timing? Maybe you were just doing your part. For the war effort.

                  Pause. MICHAEL is stunned by this.

MICHAEL: Is this a fairy tale? No. Are my reasons for loving you complicated? Maybe. But I do love you. *(He gets up to leave.)* Someone told you a long time ago that being special meant something? Well they sold you a bill of goods. You're not special to anyone but your mother and father, and maybe, if you get lucky, some poor schmuck who loves you so much he wants to marry you. And yes, Anne, I do think you're special. But not because of the goddamned attic! I hope they pave over it. I hope they make a parking lot or an empty field. Maybe then you can let it go. And see what is in front of you. *(He leaves the room.)*

ANNE gathers her things and leaves.

Scene 14

Outside of PETER's office in Toronto. ANNE and PETER stand on the street looking at each other.

PETER: Does Michael know you are here?

ANNE looks at him and shrugs. Then shakes her head, "no".

And why are you here?

ANNE: I just—I had to see you.

PETER: It's nine in the morning. You must have been on the train all night.

ANNE: I thought it would be relaxing. But it was like sitting in a dark theatre with nothing on the screen. You look out the windows and its so black in the night, you can only see your reflection.

PETER: Are you alright?

ANNE: Why does every one keep asking me that?

PETER: You're not yourself Anne.

ANNE: Not myself? No, that's true.

PETER: You're shaking—

ANNE: I'm afraid I've made some mistakes Peter. Some terrible mistakes.

PETER: What?

ANNE: I should never have let you leave my life. I should never have let you marry Betty. I should never have pushed you away.

PETER: What are you saying?

ANNE: I see it now. We belong together. I made a mistake fighting it all that time.

PETER: What about Michael?

ANNE: Yes, yes, of course I'm in love with Michael. But he doesn't understand. He can never understand, not the way that you do. I need you Peter. *(She approaches him.)* Don't you see? I need you. *(She embraces him.)* You are the only one. You are the one who believes in the story, who understands, who remembers…

PETER: Anne—

ANNE: Please. Please.

PETER steps away from her.

ANNE: Someone bought the annex. The warehouse on Prinsengracht. Someone bought it. They're tearing it down.

PETER says nothing.

I thought you said the story mattered. That you would never find it boring. If we were together…at last, then I wouldn't need the attic. I wouldn't need anything. I would be special, and so would you.

PETER: No.

ANNE: But this is what you wanted. This is what you've always wanted.

PETER: Not any more.

ANNE: Why not?

PETER: Anne. Darling Anne. Don't you see what this is doing to you? Something terrible happened. But it happened years ago. You have to let it go.

ANNE: Sometimes I think it's still happening. *(Exhausted, she sits.)* Am I crazy?

PETER: No, you're not crazy. It was still happening for me too, for a long time. I was still in the attic, still in love with you. But it was no good, you see. For anyone. I had to move on.

ANNE: Peter. What am I? I didn't die, but I didn't survive either. I've walked around for years like I was me. Like I was Anne Frank, but I wasn't me. I haven't been me in a long, long time. Anne Frank is dead. And here I am...who? Anne Stein? Who is that? A made up person I don't even know. I can't write. I can't be a voice for the millions. I can't even be a voice for myself! I can't look backward because there is too much pain, and when I try to look forward...I just can't see what I am supposed to do.

PETER: You're not supposed to do anything but live. You've been given a gift.

ANNE: A gift!

PETER: What else is it?

ANNE: But the book...the story.

PETER: *(Shrugs.)* You tried.

ANNE: I failed.

PETER: *(Shrugs again.)* Yes.

> *Pause. She looks at him.*

ANNE: I might as well have died.

PETER: Don't say that.

ANNE: Maybe they would have wanted the story then.

PETER: No.

ANNE: Why has God done this to me? Filled me with such a longing, with such a mission and given me no way to fulfill it? Why not save the rabbis and scholars and artists and mothers and sisters? They had brains and hearts and bones. Children. A million children. What about them? Who knows what they would have grown up to become? What about their stories? Why am I here if not to tell the stories? *(Beat. Realization.)* Oh Peter. It doesn't hold any water.

PETER: What?

ANNE: No reason.

PETER: What is it?

ANNE: Don't you see? No reason, Peter. No God.

PETER: Oh Anne. I don't know. Even if there is, I don't think He's up there choosing between us like kittens in a basket.

> *Pause.*

ANNE: So that's it. We suffered. We survived. We got lucky. This book doesn't really matter at all. I could just erase the words, then it would be over. *(Pause.)* But no I can't. I can't undo what happened. And no amount of words will ever make sense of it either.

> *She goes to leave.*

PETER: Where are you going?

ANNE: I have to…go. I'm sorry, Peter.

ANNE exits.

Scene 15

ANNE sits on the train platform. She takes out Kitty. Looks at her. Sets her down beside her. We hear the whistle of the train as it approaches. She takes out the pages of the manuscript. As the train approaches, the rushing air blows a page away from her. After a moment, she positions the papers so that they will all blow away. She watches them go. A transformation: Maybe it rains pages, or there is a sunrise, but something has changed. ANNE rises, and Kitty, left abandoned on the bench, waits. To be thrown out. To be discovered. ANNE leaves.

Scene 16

ANNE and PETER in PETER's study in Toronto.

ANNE: Thank you so much for dinner.

PETER: Our pleasure.

ANNE: Betty is such a wonderful cook! I am afraid Mike will never let me hear the end of it.

PETER: Not much of a cook?

ANNE: No. I get bored so easily.

PETER: Are you writing?

ANNE: Not right now. But I will.

PETER: So what have you been doing? To pass the time?

ANNE: Actually, I've been volunteering.

PETER: Volunteering, is that right?

ANNE: Yes. In the reunification office, with survivors. Children in hiding mostly. There are so many in New York.

PETER: Toronto too.

ANNE: It's been difficult of course, but it's good for me. Focusing on people other than myself. Of course we donate quite a bit of money too. It somehow never feels like enough. All those children...many people still haven't found their families, all these years later.

PETER: Terrible.

ANNE: Imagine surviving the war, the camps, and having no one left? Not a soul in the world. How lucky we were. To come through it together. It just makes me want to give and give. But Mike always says, if we gave any more we would need a handout ourselves. But you know. A person who gives is never poor.

PETER: That sounds familiar.

ANNE: Oh. Well it's just an expression. You know. Like—"Paper has more patience than people." Or—"Whoever is happy will make others happy too."

PETER: (*Thinks for a moment.*) Anne, are you quoting yourself?

ANNE: (*Pause.*) Maybe.

PETER: (*Laughs.*) You are too much.

ANNE: Well someone has to!

PETER: Really? Really someone has to?

ANNE: Oh it's nice to hear your laugh! It seems like ages since I've made you laugh. I brought you something.

> *ANNNE gives PETER a record, "The Freewheelin' Bob Dylan."*

PETER: What's this?

ANNE: It's new. You've never heard anything like it.

PETER: Oh no? How do you know that?

ANNE: Because I am the one who's given you all of your music for the past two decades, and I've never heard anything like it!

PETER: Yes, I've missed that.

ANNE: Peter, there's something else I have to tell you.

PETER: What's that?

ANNE: I am going to have a baby.

> *Pause.*

PETER: What?

ANNE: It's still early. I wasn't supposed to tell, but I am terrible with secrets.

PETER: No of course not. Congratulations!

ANNE: Yes, well. I won't be the youngest mother on the block, but it seems that everything still works as it is supposed to.

PETER: That's wonderful news. *(He hugs her.)* Michael must be so happy.

ANNE: Yes, he is. Thank you.

PETER: You'll be a wonderful mother.

ANNE: I'm not so sure.

PETER: I am.

MICHAEL and MARGOT enter laughing.

MARGOT: I thought I'd never get her to sleep. George has got her all excited about trying out snow shoes!

MICHAEL: George didn't seem to have any problem falling asleep though.

MARGOT: Well three beers! It's more than the man has drunk in his entire life.

MICHAEL: It's not just him, there's something different about this Canadian beer.

PETER: Higher alcohol content.

MICHAEL: You don't say!

PETER approaches with two cigars.

PETER: Mazel tov.

MICHAEL: Anne!

ANNE: It's Peter! I had to.

MICHAEL: Oh well, you'd have found out soon enough. *(They shake hands.)* Thank you. Say are these Cuban?

PETER: They are.

MICHAEL: How's that for a treat? It'll be a while before I see one of these again State-side.

PETER: Yes, quite a mess, that.

ANNE: Everyone's down for the night?

MARGOT: For now.

PETER: Betty's in with the boys, reading a story.

MICHAEL: Those two are something else.

MARGOT: Aren't they just darling?

PETER: Well don't be fooled. They were on their best behaviour for you tonight. They can be quite the terrors.

MICHAEL: Hope we're not too much of a disruption, dropping in like this.

PETER: Well, you were coming through Toronto. It doesn't happen everyday. So what time is your train tomorrow?

MARGOT: Nine A.M.!

PETER: Where to?

ANNE: We stop in Winnipeg. Then switch trains to Churchill.

PETER: Churchill, Manitoba. All that way just to see some bears.

ANNE: Some bears? Some bears?! They're polar bears!

MICHAEL: Don't get her started, please.

ANNE: I've been waiting my whole life!

PETER: I hope you won't be disappointed.

ANNE: Yes, well. There's no helping that. You should come along.

PETER: No, thank you. It's cold enough right here. Margot, how did your family get roped into this excursion?

MARGOT: Anne is not the only one with a sense of adventure, Peter! Perhaps you don't know everything about me. I want my children to see the world, to not miss out on a single moment.

PETER: Who knew you were so brave?

ANNE:	I knew. I knew she was brave.
MARGOT:	Oh Anne.
ANNE:	It's true. You're extraordinary. Having children alone is an act of bravery.
MARGOT:	Nonsense.
ANNE:	Well, I think so. Everything is going to change again. I'm terrified!
MARGOT:	You'll be fine.
ANNE:	How do you know?
PETER:	Because nothing in the world can break Anne Frank.
MARGOT:	That's right!
ANNE:	(*She turns to look at him.*) You called me Anne Frank! It's been a while since anyone called me that! Remember Anne Frank, Michael?
MICHAEL:	Yes, it rings a bell.
ANNE:	Anne Frank. I remember. Peter?
PETER:	Yes?
ANNE:	Do you remember the attic?
PETER:	(*He laughs.*) I do.
ANNE:	It was awful wasn't it?
PETER:	Yes, it was.
ANNE:	Sometimes I miss it.
MARGOT:	That's just your mind playing tricks on you.
ANNE:	No, I know it was a terrible time. That we were hungry and cold and terribly afraid all the time.

I know that. I remember it. But it's not what I feel when I think about it. When I think about it, I feel hope. *(The lights begin to fade on the rest of the stage.)* And not just the hope that we would survive, but hope for the whole world. Hope for the rest of my life in front of me. I always thought with that extraordinary beginning...I guess I just thought things would turn out a little more extraordinary. *(ANNE stands in a spotlight, with only the faintest hint of the others behind her.)* But it doesn't matter really. I suppose, not everything happens for a reason. But that doesn't mean life is without meaning. Maybe life, just life, just being alive is remarkable enough. It is, isn't it? Yes. After everything, I understand. Life is spectacular. Just the way it is.

"A Hard Rain's Gonna Fall" by Bob Dylan plays as the lights go down.

Blackout.

The End.